THE ART AND CR.
OF FRENCH I

H. Crosbie

ARTHUR H. STOCKWELL LTD.
Elms Court   Ilfracombe
Devon

ISBN 0 7223 2102-3

Printed in Great Britain by
Arthur H. Stockwell Ltd.
Elms Court   Ilfracombe
Devon

CONTENTS

Foreword	5
Introduction	7
Timbers	11
Inlaid Work, Cross-Banding, Strings, Etc.	12
Types of Stains	13
Advice on Mahogany Staining	16
Advice on Walnut Staining	17
Filling In	18
Filling In Notes	19
How to Improve Mahogany	19
Making a Fad	20
Fadding Up	21
Bodying Up	24
Illustrations In Making a Rubber	25
Art of Spiriting Off	27
Spiriting Only	28
Sulphuric Piano Acid Finish	28
Bleaching	30
Stopping and Bruises	31
Colouring	31
Ebonising	33
General Hints	34
Stripping	36
Old Furniture, Repaired and Polished	38
Types of Polish	39
Varnishing and Types of Varnish	40
Advice and Defects	41
Antique Restoration	47
Reproduction of Antique Oak	47
Oak Colouring and Staining	48
Doctoring and First Aid	49
Spirit and Solid Colours	50
Lacquers and Synthetics	51
Types of Lacquer	52
Revivers	53
Cellulose Finishing	54
Terms Used In French Polishing	54
Terms and Materials	55
Manufacturer's address	63

FOREWORD

I have no hesitation in recommending this book for learners or semi-craftsmen, as it is advantageous to know that here you have a wealth of fifty years practical experience on all wood finishes, entirely on French Polishing, taking the reader progressively through every stage of the work step by step. As this book covers all the invaluable source of information on finishing all kinds of woodwork — with trade secrets, that has been handed down from father to son, to accomplish a first-class tradesman of professional craftsmanship. As it is only personal experience with finishing, that will enable you to make a great success of your workmanship, also patience and experiments in various stages such as preparing, staining, filling in, fadding, colouring, coating, bodying, stiffing, spiriting out, and finally the Sulphuric Acid finish. All these processes will take place as you follow through.

French Polishing is the art of laying layers of thin film of polish on a surface, by means of a rubber, on veneers and exotic hardwoods to beautify a long lasting silk finish, as a number of enthusiasts consider this something of a crowning achievement; especially with a beautiful glass finish as you see on a grand piano; as with this special glass, mirror finish (as we call this in the trade), as a Sulphuric Acid finish. This I will explain at a later stage in the book. Therefore, here you have an invaluable handbook which will give the reader a sound, practical foundation of good French Polishing on all types of woods.

5

Introduction (by H. Crosbie)

The purpose of this book is to show you the way to craftsmanship — not by the way of a road map!

As you don't have to be a Master of Science to learn and understand the secret techniques of this trade, I will explain step by step the simple self-improvement programme; how a good DIY semi-craftsman, or an enthusiastic layman, with care and patience, can master the art of professional French Polishing. It will take time and patience, as like all trades, one must start at the bottom rung of the ladder.

Therefore, the object of my book is based on years of experience which has been handed down from father to son over the generations when French Polishers have been the cream of craftsmanship in every way — proud and devoted to his workmanship.

French Polishing has several advantages as stated — moneywise, pride, and a master of craftsmanship. At times I've been called a magician, as people would ask me if I could bring this old piece of furniture back to life again which they have treasured, especially if it is inherited, or a sentimental piece of furniture. So this is where your skill starts.

Firstly you repair it, then strip it (if necessary), and prepare the groundwork to stain, colour and French Polish. What an achievement to bring it back to its original condition — that's magic with pride and craftsmanship. Also, you can name your own price, as there are only a few craftsmen who can do this kind of work.

This book is of great value and interest to the needs of a home ownership who takes part in DIY and is prepared to invest time and great effort in persevering to renovate his furniture in fine condition. Therefore, if the owner-restorer is prepared to invest a

7

great amount of his time in learning the skills involved in renovation, he will also come into contact with good class cabinet-making practice, to dismantle a faulty piece of furniture and reassemble it correctly, instead of carrying out a botch job of it. At the same time he will encounter the skill of French Polishing to complete his job of interest. But to gain knowledge and experience in buying furniture to work on, handle and take apart, then rebuild it to its natural state; one must venture into auction rooms and junk shops. You will be surprised what you can find even in attics!

Before you begin work, the first problem is to assess what needs to be done. You must be able to tell what has gone wrong with it, and you must judge how far it needs to be dismantled. All of these problems can be overcome with experience and practice in know-how. So, to gain experience with furniture, have confidence in carrying out restoration, and to handle furniture yourself, spend a considerable amount of time thoughtfully examining the job. Be patient, as knowledge and skill is not achieved overnight; so be practicable, because pride comes from personal achievement and organisation. Have all the necessary tools required — your chisels nicely sharpened, several grades of glass-papers, various sizes of cramps.

Most craftsmen find in refinishing and repairing, a great pleasure, a rewarding job and most satisfying, especially on old antique work, where you have to judge on complicated repair work. Sometimes problems occur even with the professional restorer and one has to weigh up the pros and cons. It's a challenge of know-how in regards to the amount of time it takes to repair; how far to strip it (if needed), or dismantle; and can he find the right veneer or hardwoods to replace? Therefore, this is where the experience, skill and craftsmanship comes into play; also to charge the correct fee and expenses. In my opinion, for a young man to take up professional French Polishing and repair work, can be a very rewarding profession as French Polishers will be very scarce to come by in a few years. However, once the home polisher, or amateur, practice and experiment on the basis of this procedure which I have given in this book step by step, then he will accomplish his achievement, and produce a perfectly acceptable high finish to his requirements. But have patience and confidence in yourself, that you will become a successful French Polisher. Also, it is important to arrange certain workshop conditions: i.e., a reasonably warm temperature and dust-free room or workshop. Central heating is ideal, with the temperature above 65 degrees in Fahrenheit; otherwise, if your workshop is cold and damp, the

French Polish is liable to chill (turning slightly green). A good practice when polishing is to arrange your job with the light facing you, then you can see the smear of oil working when polishing.

I will now proceed in the skill and art of French Polishing, which is without doubt the most challenging, refined art of finishes on all types of hardwoods, veneers and antiques. Nowadays, furniture is finished with either cellulose, lacquer or polyurethane, which looks very synthetic.

But to deal with hardwoods, one can repair it, strip it and French Polish, and without doubt it brings out the beauty in woods. So, to be a good French Polisher one must know the basics of woods and veneers, such as English Oak, American Walnut, Burmese Teak, Indian Rosewood and Brazilian, Tulipwood, Zebrano, Sycamore, Satinwood, Tola Honduras and Brazilian Mahogany, Jacobean Dark Oak, etc.

First Stage in French Polishing

Before you attempt to polish your job, look it over, especially if it's a new job which you have made yourself. Make sure that there are no glue or finger marks or bruises. If so, paper down with number one sandpaper — make sure your job is nice and clean. Then you start off with the choice of staining, fadding up, colouring, then finish off with your rubber charged with polish. I will proceed in various stages, step by step, so as to learn and master the art of polishing.

TIMBERS

This actually comes under carpentry, but I can only give you my own personal experience on this.

However, if the amateur or carpenter has made a sideboard or table, then groundwork is essential. If the job is veneered by yourself, then make sure that all finger and glue marks are scraped out by a sharp scraper. Then give it a good clean-up with various grades of sandpaper, as veneers and solid woods must be thoroughly prepared — most carpenters know this. As for the amateur to use a scraper, always hold it at an angle at askew, so that the blade rests firmly upon the wood, and push the blade away from you. Sometimes, you may come across some woods with woolly textures, then you have to coax the job. Work one way and the other way. You must give this your undivided attention.

Glass-papering

Now is the stage where you look over the job for plane marks or minor imperfections caused by your scraper. Therefore, to remove these, use a flat cork to level off, starting with No. 1½ grade in sandpaper, and finally finish with No. 1 and No. 0. On working with deal wood, a carpenter only uses sandpaper and not a scraper — being a softwood.

Veneers

As you know, veneers are not planed, only scraped and sandpapered. I explained that all the glue marks must be removed. This is an important factor, but be very careful in scraping and papering as one is liable to go through the veneers. With some veneers such as Birds Eye Maple, Burr Maple and Burr Walnut, use only No. 1 sandpaper to start off with. Work lightly with a circular movement and finish off with fine flour paper. With regard to woods that have been machine planed, it is advisable to wash it down with hot water to raise the grain, then paper down when dry. The same procedure is used on mouldings.

Mouldings

It is a good practice to paper down and polish mouldings before being fitted to the job — the same applies to a four drawer chest — take off all handles and fittings, pull out drawers so that a nice clean job can be attained.

Natural Woods

These should not be stained or coloured, as it must be as natural as possible. But, if the individual requires it in a richer state, then apply linseed oil (raw) and white mineral oil mixed equally, and wash it with these oils, but it must be wiped off thoroughly, papered down with fine flour paper and wiped off with a soft piece of cloth. Now prepare to fad up with white polish and finish with transparent polish. Wax polish can also be used on natural wood; wash in with white polish, paper down, and give two coats of white polish. After it is dry, then apply wax finish.

These exotic veneers may surprise people to know that veneering was used some 3,000 years ago by the Egyptians, and also by the Ancient Greeks and Romans. Although Walnut veneer was mostly used during the reign of William and Mary — but the master craftsmen such as Chippendale, Hepplewhite veneered in Mahogany, Burr Yew and Satinwood; although the modern craftsmen have revived some of the ancient crafts. Therefore, if the younger generation don't trouble to learn these crafts and skills by the older craftsmen, the skills will die with them, and all will be lost.

INLAID WORK, CROSS-BANDING, STRINGS, ETC.

With most old Mahogany sideboards of Sheraton style or Hepplewhite period, they have exotic veneers rich in colour of Burr Yew and Mahogany. Amboyna woods, decorated with delicate marquetry and cross-banding; strings; boxwood lines of Tulipwood, Ebony, Macassar, Satinwood inlaid — mostly used on classical furniture. Therefore, on this kind of high-class furniture you have some dedicated work to perform in sealing the strings, cross-banding and boxwood lines. This can be accomplished by using a soft long bristle pencil or artists' brush. This process must be carried out quickly and carefully. Either cellulose lacquer, or white polish is used to seal the strings, etc. I would recommend cellulose lacquer to use, as oil stains, water and spirit stains will not effect it. Two coats must be applied of cellulose or white polish to seal it, and great care must be taken not to go over onto the Mahogany veneer. When the coating is completed, stain with a weak Bichromate of Potash (water stain), dilute with water if required. Drying time is very important on this kind of work. Give the sealing, in one or two hours hours — water staining of Bichromate 12-24 hours. Occasionally, a polisher comes across a Mahogany sideboard that has to be stripped with exotic veneers, strings, cross-banding, etc. Then, use a good brand of chemical stripper 'Jaxastryp' (address at the back of book). This will not affect the colour. Always purchase the best materials on good class work, and fill in with a good Mahogany paste filler which has a slight colouring in. But firstly don't forget to seal the Bichromate stain when dry with two coats of garnet polish. Fad up with this polish, but don't go too far with it, then finish off with special pale transparent polish. Another point I would like to mention on stripping your job is to look it over and if the cross-banding or strings are a bit proud (lifted up), wrap a piece of sandpaper, No. 0, around the finger and paper down lightly, don't use a block. Also, on fadding you notice that some parts of the strings and banding have lifted up, as sometimes it cannot be seen on bare wood, as all faults show up after a few coats of polish have been applied. Therefore, the tricks of the trade apply here: wipe over the high parts with white vaseline oil and level down with a piece of glass-paper wrapped around the finger as mentioned; then wipe off the affected parts.

Note: Before staining with Bichromate stain, always wash the job down with warm water to raise the grain. When dried off, paper down smoothly and stain.

TYPES OF STAIN

Water Stains

These stains are best to use, although they take longer in drying time, but they are cheap and non-fading and ensure a nice even tone with an even penetration over a large area. Also, water stain powder can be purchased in a great variety of colours. When adding powder stain to mix with warm water, allow a good hour before using, as some ingredients take longer to dissolve. Allow about 12 hours or more before coating (sealing). One disadvantage with water stains is that they are liable to raise the grain, therefore one must wash down the job with hot or warm water *before staining,* then allow to dry and sand down with medium glass-paper, and dust down. Some stain powder leaves a film of sediment. To overcome this, strain through a piece of butter muslin before using.

Spirit Stains

This is a stain powder soluble in methylated spirits and has the advantage of drying quickly. Also, they are not liable to raise the grain of wood, although experience is needed to stain a large area as speed is essential in applying and wiping off. Spirit stains are very useful to a self-employed polisher as time is saved. Also, it has a good penetration on old finishes as this can be applied immediately after the stripping process. When using spirit stains always add a touch of French Polish to act as a binder. It only takes 10-15 minutes to dry before sealing.

Oil Stains

These are powder dyes dissolved in any light oil such as naphtha, turps, benzolene or similar oils (in a variety of colours), and this stain can be purchased ready-mixed in liquid form, but these do not have the same penetration as water or spirit stains, although they are ideal for a quick colour stain. When dry, seal with two coats of French Polish.

Oil Finish

Oil polishing is an old fashioned method, mostly obsolete, but has the advantage over French Polishing as there is no danger of the surface cracking up, blooming or blistering. It gives a hard oil finish on close grain wood. Oil polishing is hard work and patience is essential as several applications of oil have to be rubbed in hard, and it can take up to a year to complete; but the surface will resist heat and water marks.

Varnish Stain

This is mostly used to stain floors and is not used in professional polishing. It is, however, sometimes used in home making furniture as a cheap, quick refinish.

Mahogany Staining to Walnut

Most polishers use Green Copperas to tone down Mahogany to resemble Walnut. This takes out the redness in Mahogany, but be very cautious as it is a very powerful stain. Green Copperas is of a crystal nature and can easily be made up by dissolving the crystals in warm water, but always test your stain on a piece of wood of the same nature. It is advisable to make it weak at first as if the stain is too strong it will form an 'Air Force' blue. To mix Green Copperas, add a teaspoon full of this crystal to a pint of warm water. This can be thinned down if too strong by adding more water, or strengthened by adding more crystals. When dry, seal it with two coats of white polish.

Walnut Water Stain

Use vandyke crystals, mix with warm water, the same mixture as above. Also, .880 ammonia can be added (about a tablespoonful). This can make the stain more penetrating but of a slightly darker shade. Ammonia .880 can be used in all water stains if required. *Note* that with water staining always wash in your job with hot or warm water. (See Staining notes).

Black Ebony Stain

This can easily be made up by adding a teaspoonful of spirit black aniline powder to ½ pint of methylated spirit and a dash of French Polish, then polish with Black Ebony polish. This can be obtained already made up.
Note: On mixing crystals or aniline powders with water or methylated spirits on staining, it is advisable to strain through a piece of muslin to get rid of grit or sediment.

Aniline Powder Dyes

These can be obtained in several colours; Bismark Brown, Vandyke

Brown, Red, Green, Purple, Maroon, to suit all colouring requirements. However, be very cautious when mixing as they are very powerful stains. Keep the powders in an airtight jar and label individually. When mixed with water add vinegar to bind it, a dash of French Polish if mixed with methylated spirit, and turpentine for oil stain. Test your stains first on a piece of wood of the same material before staining the original job.

Ammonia

This is of a liquid form. Take great care when using this — wear rubber gloves as it bites into the skin, and wear protective eye glasses. Ammonia is of great value for mixing in with water stains, it has a great effect for penetrating the stain deeply into the grain. It does, however, have the effect of darkening the wood slightly, so use it very sparingly.

The amateur can gain a lot of knowledge with stains, knowing the correct stain to use and the correct mixture. This can cut down time in colouring to match his original job, especially if the polisher is self-employed as he has to judge and weigh up the pros and cons for the quickest method to save time and money on his customer's side. One cannot charge his customer 12 hours waiting time for water stains to dry thoroughly, therefore the polisher has to use either spirit or oil stains. It depends on how big the job is, or if there is other work for the polisher to concentrate on, to allow for the use of water stain to be used.

ADVICE ON MAHOGANY STAINING

Before proceeding to stain with Bichromate of Potash on Mahogany or other woods, always wash down with warm water so as to raise the grain of the job. When it is dry, paper down the grain to obtain a smooth surface, then the job can be stained with Bichromate. It is advisable to mix it with warm water, not cold, and add about a tablespoonful of Ammonia (.880) to stain, for penetration.

Mahogany staining can be toned to different varieties which improves its richness. However, Spanish and Cuban Mahogany does not require to be stained. This timber is very rare nowadays — it is expensive. It is very rich in colour especially when linseed oil is applied as a mild stain of natural colour.

However, the most successful rich stain to use on Mahogany is

Bichromate of Potash. This is a water stain which brings out the beauty on woods. It is a very strong red stain, so be careful that your job does not become too red. It can be diluted with water according to the strength required. A good plan is to mix a little Mahogany stain with Walnut stain (Vandyke crystals). Use a medium strength, but always try out your stains on a spare piece of the same wood or underneath the job. A good idea, if the colour on your job is not the deep red required, is to allow the Bichromate stain to dry thoroughly, then rub down with fine flour paper and restain with medium Mahogany oil stain. This will eliminate going over again with Bichromate stain and save a lot of drying time.

ADVICE ON WALNUT STAINING

Walnut is a beautiful natural wood that rarely needs staining. Some polishers just apply linseed oil over the job to bring out a rich tone. To do this proceedure just oil in all over the job with a pad of cotton wool, then wipe off the excessive oil, paper down with fine flour paper and wipe off again. Then start fadding up. Do not use any oil as you have enough on the job as the fad will work out the oil. In this case no filling is required as the grain will gradually fill up with polish.

Walnut Staining

If staining is required on Walnut then use Vandyke Crystals. This is a water stain that gives Walnut a dark brown colour, but use it weak. If too strong, dilute with water, or distilled water, and try out the stain on a spare piece of the same wood. Certain Walnut have a variety of different veneers from that of solid parts. To overcome this a certain amount of colouring has to be accomplished in the polishing process, but stain first. Sometimes a polisher may come across a job with Mahogany solid woods with Walnut veneers. Now this is where a certain amount of skill comes into play. This happens sometimes on polished doors as the Mahogany shows up more when stripped. Therefore, to kill the red, one must stain with Green Copperas. This can easily be made up by dissolving the crystals in water, but test this on a piece of timber first. Make up a teaspoonful of crystals to a pint of water, it can be diluted or strengthened according to the shade required. When dry it will be of a blue shade. Seal the stain with a couple of coats of white French Polish. Do not use Copperas Crystal stain on *deep red Mahogany* as it is unsuitable.

With regard to water stains, these are best to use as they have the capacity to cover a wider surface per gallon and are relatively cheap. They also have a wide variety of colours in powder form that can be purchased at the polish manufacturers (address at back of book). It is a very rewarding and interesting job to be able to mix up your own colours, and matching up to the required colour. Some polishers apply the stain with a brush, others with wadding or rag.

FILLING IN

Most hard timbers such as Mahogany, Walnut, Sycamore, Satinwood, etc., need not be filled in, as one can fill in the grain with polish, by giving the job a good fadding up and cut down with fine flour paper. This can save a lot of time.

The main purpose of filling in is to seal the grain of open timber. Plaster of Paris is the oldest filler in use. This is cheap and effective, as the superfine grade used can be purchased at any oil shop — it is easily obtained. There are several fillers on the market, and home-made fillers too. Wheeler's is a good filler — this brand is mostly sold by polishing suppliers and can be obtained in a variety of colours to match your job. It is supplied in various size tins. To use Wheeler's filler, one must thin this paste filler down with Turpentine to the required strength — thick, thin or medium paste.

Filling in with Plaster of Paris has advantages; it is cheap to purchase, it is a very hard filler and is easy to use. A piece of canvas is ideal to use or a thick piece of open rag. Put the Plaster in an open, shallow box, and a bowl of water by the side of it. Wet up your canvas or rag, make a pad of it, then dip it in Plaster and rub into the job in a circular movement. Apply pressure on the canvas. If it is too wet, dip in Plaster again to obtain a nice thick paste and rub well in; also across the grain. Allow the Plaster a few seconds to dry to set, but not too long as it hardens very quickly. Then rub off very briskly across the grain. Great care should be taken to clean off a section at a time. Use a clean piece of canvas each time as the canvas or rag gets choked up with filler. Where mouldings and corners get choked up, clean out with a sharp ended wooden stick and brush out with a stiff brush. Allow the whole job to dry thoroughly until the surface has turned white. Soak a piece of wadding into a bowl of raw linseed oil and cover the job all over with a film of oil. Then, paper the job thoroughly all over as you will find that the oil on the surface will form as a thin paste. When the whole of the surface has been papered, wipe off with a clean, soft rag, and repeat. However, on light woods and natural Walnut, use white oil instead of linseed oil, as white oil is colourless.

Colouring Plaster Of Paris

Should the individual require to fill in Mahogany or Walnut, then one must mix colour powders with the Plaster. Use Rose Pink powder for Mahogany and Vandyke Brown powder for Walnut. Also, one can mix the two powders with Plaster if required.

FILLING IN NOTES

When using patent filler, and allowing for drying time, it is advisable to give it a paper down with No. 1 sandpaper before proceeding to polish, as this will take off any excess filler that has been left on. This also applies to Plaster of Paris — take care that no small nibs of filler are left in the corners.

With Plaster of Paris filled and oiled in, make sure that the linseed oil is well wiped off. There will, however, be a small amount of oil left in the job. To overcome this use your fad straight up and down two or three times. Use polish only on fad, no oil, as this will enable you to get a thin film of polish onto the surface and it also takes out the remaining oil.

For the individual who would like to mix up their own Paste Filler, it is as follows:

>   1 quart of boiled Linseed Oil
>   1 pint of Gold Size or Brown Japan
>   1 gill of Turpentine

Also, add China Clay or Silex to mix in with the ingredients.

HOW TO IMPROVE MAHOGANY

To be richer in colour, and bring out the full beauty of a rich grain, one must use Bichromate of Potash crystals. These are reddish crystals which you mix with water. First, heat the water up. Then add about a tablespoonful of crystals — 2 pints warm water — but be careful, as the crystals are very strong. You vary the amount of crystals to your strength or tone required for the job; mix up well. If you think it is too strong add more water to it to weaken. Before staining your job it is a good tip to wet the job all over first with warm water, then allow it to dry. Now this will raise the grain of the wood, then when dry give it a good papering down with No. 1 glass-paper and again with fine paper. Also, you may need to use fine flour paper so the job is nice and smooth, and dust it down well. Now your job is ready for staining. But, before you start, put a pair of rubber gloves on as the Bichromate bites in to your skin. If you get it on your hands it will take a few days to get the colour stain off, but it is not dangerous to use. However, you can use either a pad of wadding or rag. If you are staining a table top or a flat surface, a good tip is to start at the bottom of the job with the grain of wood and work up to the top (as shown).

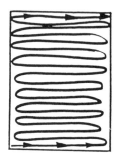

Work from left to right evenly, then wipe off evenly with the grain and repeat with a clean piece of rag, but allow 12 hours drying time before polishing.

MAKING A FAD

Have a piece of wadding some 9 inches square. Then fold it in half, then again; now pour some methylated spirit onto the pad of wadding — not too much — then lightly shape it around in your hands to make it pear-shaped, then flatten it on the back of a piece of glass-paper and wring out well of spirit. Then leave it for about 10 minutes to dry off and shape it conveniently to fit your hand, and charge the fad of wadding with polish. Use Garnet Polish to fad up on Mahogany so as to see the true colour of the Bichromate stain. After your first coat of polish leave it to dry for about 10 minutes, then paper down with fine flour paper and dust down after. Now your job should be nice and smooth, so repeat. To give it another coat of polish, you may need to charge your fad up again with Garnet Polish and flatten your fad again on a piece of glass-paper (back). Always do this when charging up with polish either on a fad or rubber, as this serves the purpose of evenly distributing the polish all over the surface of your job. Now after two or three coats of polish on the job, when dry, you start to look over the job which we call 'preparing' — you fill in small holes with a colour wax with a penknife. All these materials you can purchase from the polishing manufacturer whose address is at the back of the book. When preparing, if the job is bruised you can put a small amount of methylated spirit in the bruised hole, then light the methylate, but be careful, it will then burn out the bruise it will raise. Then, paper off level and fad one coat of polish, then recolour the bruised part.

FADDING UP

This fadding is only the preliminary stage of the polishing process, which is called 'ground work' in the trade. Therefore, after staining and sealing it with two or three coats of polish (no oil), then preparing in filling up holes, etc., we come to the fadding process.

Now up to the present no oil has been used so as to ensure that the timber has been completely sealed. However, to build up a good groundwork, you use a little oil on your fad. So, dip up your fad with polish, and smear a little oil on the fad with your finger. Start off with straight strokes across the surface (see figure A) two or three times, then smear a little oil on the fad again to give it a more free movement, and work the fad around in an anti-clockwise movement in wide open circles (as shown in figures B & C), but don't forget the corners. When fadding, should you get a piece of wadding stuck on the surface, stop immediately — allow yourself a minute — then dip your finger in the linseed oil and rub the wadding off; it will come away on your finger. Also, if you see pimples form on the surface caused by dust then it should be slightly eased off with a piece of old oily flour paper. When the job is nice and clean, straighten up with fad. Also, in fadding, if you see a nice smear on the surface, then you know you have the correct amount of oil and polish. This will come to you with practice. If you find your fad or rubber gets too dry, dip up again with polish, and if more oil is required then sprinkle it on the surface. But, if you keep on adding too much oil to the fad or rubber, it will become too greasy; also it will choke up the rag. When you find that you have a good foundation of polish on the surface of your job after fadding up, use your rubber to take out the remaining oil left on the job. Charge your rubber with polish and flatten on the back of the sandpaper to even out the polish, and just smear a little oil on the surface of the rubber to start it off, and glide straight across the job so as to prevent it from sticking. Do this three or four times, then work gently around in large circles. Straighten up several times if you feel your rubber getting a bit dry, then add some pressure on the rubber as this will help to get the oil out quicker, but don't hurry the job by using too wet rubbers or the oil will be buried. Also, if too much oil is used it sometimes clogs up the rag which will *not* give the pulling effect on the rubber. So, change the rag and apply a new piece. Always work in a well-lit room as a better view can be attained to see the smear of oil working on the surface.

The Procedure Stages on Fadding

A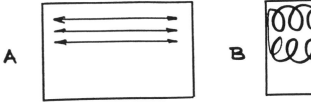

Straight, even strokes.

B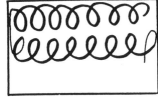

Work round and round, large circles anti-clockwise.

C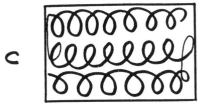

Work in corners, large circle in the middle.

D

Work against grain as fig.8 and straighten off.

Bodying Up Process

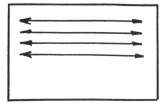

Straight, even strokes.

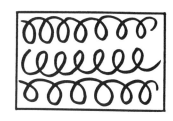

Work round and round in large circles anti-clockwise.

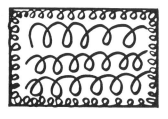

Work in corners and large circles in the middle.

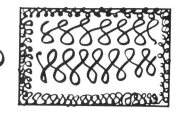

Figure of eight movement.

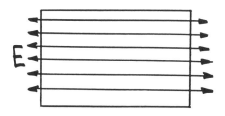

Straight, long strokes straight off ends (stiffing off).

BODYING UP

This is a very important progress in French Polishing. Therefore, I would advise the amateur to carry out certain workshop conditions with central heating — with a temperature just above 65 degrees Fahrenheit — in a dust-free room or workshop. Dust can do quite an amount of damage to a polished surface, as it can tear up and cause nibs or pips. Should this happen, then stop immediately, allow to dry for 15 minutes, then paper down lightly with an old oily piece of flour paper. However, most expert French Polishers have a routine in bodying up, but some have a variation on the basic process, as on fadding up. A polisher may prefer to use a rubber, another a fad, working in with linseed oil. It depends on how expert you are. Now, for bodying up, make sure your fadding up is nice and flat. Give it a good papering down and dust down well. Start off first with your rubber charged with polish, always dab your rubber on the back of glass-paper as this will distribute the polish evenly in the rubber. Should the rubber be over-charged with polish, press on the rubber to squeeze out the excessive polish.

Apply the rubber onto the surface, glide it on with straight strokes to begin with, then sprinkle some linseed oil on the surface and smear the oil on the rubber that remains on your finger. Go over the surface three or four times in a straight swing lightly. After the straight movements, you work round and round anti-clockwise, applying a slight pressure on the rubber. On circling the surface two or three times, straighten up now and then, otherwise ring marks will show up. Apply pressure on the rubber as the polish is being worked in. Then, as the rubber tends to get dry, move the rubber in a figure of eight movement (see figure D), varying your strokes and movements. Dip up polish now and then, as the rubber feels dry. You will find that to obtain a full grain finish, you must dip up (charge) your rubber several times with polish, but use the linseed oil very sparingly. The oil is used to lubricate so that the polish can be worked into the grain of the wood. For the amateur, I would advise to practice on an odd piece of veneered wood, preferably on a large scale, because it will give you more time to work the oil out with more experience.

Keep your rubber in an airtight tin or jar, and keep your grinding rubber (charged with Pumice Powder) separate from the polishing rubbers.

ILLUSTRATIONS IN MAKING A RUBBER

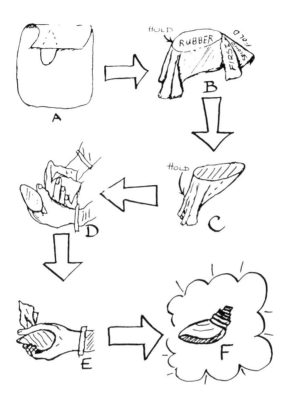

Proceed with a piece of rag 9″ square and place it face down (as in figure A). Hold the rubber at the end (as shown in figure B). Make two folds under the rubber (as in figure B and C). Hold the rubber in the left hand at the end and pull the rag taut. Screw up the ends of rag by the right hand (as in figure D) anti-clockwise and place the ends of the rag between the finger and thumb of the right hand. With the fingers, hold the rubber at the point end, and tuck the rag ends in the palm of the right hand as this is now ready to use. The rubber should look as in figure F.

Making The Rubber

To make your rubber, you need some cotton wadding about 9″ square and charge it with Methylated spirit just enough to wet it all over. Then place it in your hands and mould it into the shape like a pumice stone or pear shape, so as to obtain a nice point in the front of it. Leave it for about 10-15 minutes for the Methylated spirits to dry off. Then obtain a nice clean piece of cotton or linen cloth. Now the type of cloth is very important to a craftsman as it must be *white* — no coloured textures or pattern cloth, otherwise the dyes could *seep through* on to the work. Old, worn pillow cases, mens' white handkerchiefs, old linen or cotton white shirts, are ideal materials. I would recommend good Irish linen, as the weave is just right — not too open. However, now back to making a rubber. As you have soaked up the wadding and left it to dry off a bit and shaped it into a pad, obtain a piece of clean white rag about 9″ square. Place this face down on your bench or table about 3-4″ from the front of the rag, more to the left. Lap the front of rag over the wadding (see figure 1), then pick up the rubber by your left hand with the rag hanging down, now pull the rag *taut* at the point of rubber, with the finger and thumb of right hand, still holding the end (heel) of rubber by your left hand; now pull the rag under the rubber toward the end. Tuck the rag under the thumb of left hand whilst still holding at the end. This is your first fold. Now repeat the action again to make your second fold. Hold tight the end of rubber by your left hand with the ends of rag between the finger and thumb, now grip the whole of rubber by your right hand tightly, and turn the rubber clockwise still holding tight at the ends to the rag. Then tuck the ends at the back of rubber, as this will mould into the palm of your hand. As an amateur this is not easy to make a rubber, but practice and patience are the key points on this, as it may take two to six months to make a craftsman's polish rubber.

However, having made your rubber, you can flatten this out on the back of glass-paper to squeeze out the excessive Methylated spirit left in the rubber (this will also shape it), then pull back the rag to charge up with polish. Always hold the heel (back) of rubber by your left hand as this gives your right hand the freedom to pull the rag back, also to dip up with polish. When applying the rubber to the surface of the job, always glide it on and off as this prevents the rubber from sticking on the polished surface. Use the motion of a swinging action to start the job, then gradually increase the pressure on the rubber as it gets a bit dry, then circle round and round, straightening up from time to time. Always put your rubbers and fads in an airtight tin or plastic bag, but screw the ends up and tie a knot.

Another good point, always remember to pull back the rag on your rubber to recharge with polish or Methylated spirit as it is a bad practice to apply the polish straight on to the rag as it can easily get choked up. A good practice is to loosen up the wadding in the rubber from time to time and this will allow the polish to soak in evenly. Also, change the rag occasionally. Should it get greasy or choked up, wash it out in Methylated spirit.

THE ART OF SPIRITING OFF

Before proceeding with spiriting off, take an old hard rubber, soak it up well with Methylated spirit and wash out the remaining polish in the rubber — let it dry off for 10 minutes. Then, mix half Methylated spirit with half of colourless transparent polish in a pint bottle. Now you are ready for the actual work.

To summarize the work that has been carried out, you have bodied up a full grain finish and cut down with worn, oiled, fine flour paper free of pimples, so that you have a nice clean job. Now proceed to dip up your rubber with half and half of polish and Meths; sprinkle some linseed oil on the surface of the job and spread a little oil on your rubber. Start off with straight strokes, glide the rubber on and off using a swinging action. After several straight strokes of the rubber now change your movement into large circles anti-clockwise, and do not forget the corners. Now your rubber should be drying out a bit, so put some pressure on the rubber; work an even pressure, more so on inward swing of the circle; now your rubber should be pulling slightly, so gradually increase the pressure as the rubber gets drier. Add a little more oil if required so as to get the smear correctly the full width of the rubber; carry on progressing; dip up more polish when required.

After circles, change to a figure of eight movement. Then straighten up with the rubbing going on and off the surface. The amateur needs a lot of judgement as to when to dip up with the polish, and how much oil is required; but with practice and patience you can master it. But in circling the surface two or three times, straighten up now and then, otherwise you will get circle marks on the surface.

SPIRITING ONLY

This follows on from spiriting off. Take an old rubber, wash out with Methylated spirit as explained earlier, or obtain some medical cotton wool as a substitute for wadding. It is ideal for spiriting off, as it automatically hardens when you dip up. Now you have dipped up with Methylated spirit only (no polish), only damp the surface of rubber — do not flood it — cover the rubber with a piece of damask table-cloth (if you can obtain it). If not, use a fine soft textured linen and keep your rubber in a separate airtight jar or clean tin. To test the correct amount of spirits in the rubber, hold it to your lips. It will feel cold and sharp as then it is just right. If too dry, sprinkle some spirit on a clean piece of white rag, and wipe the rubber across it. Make sure that the spirit rubber is not too wet as it will take off the oil too quickly, and will tend to burn the polish. Start off with long straight strokes, then large circles, then back to the figure of eight movement; straighten up on long strokes on and off the surface. Continue with this procedure until the oil smear has disappeared and looks like a mirror finish.

Finally, dip the face of rubber into a bowl of Vienna Chalk and work in long strokes to burnish the surface to free any traces of oil smears. There is an art in spiriting off to attain that special mirror-like finish, but it can be achieved by careful procedure and patience.

Now the next procedure after spiriting, is the Sulphuric Acid process, more so used on piano polishing, as follows:

SULPHURIC PIANO ACID FINISH

Here we have a finish which is known in the trade as a Sulphuric Acid Finish which is of a very high-class standard, and which gives a mirror glass high shine. Now this must be a full grain highly polished finish of great quality. Therefore, to polish a piano one must go through the following building-up processes such as staining, filling, fadding, colouring, then finally the bodying operation and finishing a full grain polished surface. The acid finish can only be accomplished by giving your job a 24 hour period for drying time. Therefore, the job is now ready to proceed with. Make sure your surface is clean and free from pimples and dust.

Now mix up your Sulphuric Acid; mix this acid in cold water, or distilled water is best, but always use rubber gloves when mixing. There is a secret in mixing the two together. Firstly, obtain a thick or strong pint bottle which is clear. Fill it with ½ pint of distilled water, hold the bottle in the left hand and pour the Sulphuric Acid *very, very slowly* into the water until you feel the bottle getting warm, then stop; but you must pour the acid in very slowly so as to give it time to mix with the water — then you should have the correct mixture — that is my own secret.

The other method is to mix seven parts of distilled, or cold water, to the one part of Sulphuric Acid. When mixing, always add the acid to the water and shake up well. Then pour some of the mixture onto the face of the muslin cloth. But first have a Pounce Bag ready (as shown) filled with Vienna Chalk.

Precipitated Chalk can also be used as a substitute. Apply the acid mixture to the surface of the polished job with the muslin cloth; but should you get any pitting, or pock marks of chalk appear on the surface of your job, then the mixture is *too strong*. Therefore it should be diluted with cold water or distilled, as if this mixture is too strong, it is liable to affect the colouring of the job. The next procedure after applying the mixture of Sulphuric Acid is to use a Pounce Bag, as follows:

So now to the final finish after your job has been coloured and spirited out. I would advise you to do all these preparations on a nice piece of veneered Mahogany or Walnut wood — a large piece, so as to give you more experience before trying out on pianos or furniture. The next step is to make or obtain a Pounce Bag, as we call it in the trade (see illustration). This is filled with fine Vienna Chalk and dabbed and patted onto the surface of the job. The bag is of muslin, made up just like your mother would make a plum duff pudding, but with Vienna Chalk inside, and a piece of string tied around the top of the bag. If one cannot obtain Vienna Chalk use Precipitated Chalk. Now have a piece of muslin or soft rag and make it up into a pad. Then pour your mixture of water and Sulphuric Acid onto the pad (not too wet) and proceed in laying it onto the surface straight with the grain

Pounce Bag

lightly. Then pick up your Pounce Bag and pat it all over the job so that the chalk escapes through the mesh of the muslin and lays on the surface. Next, burnish up the work with the palm of the hand, working from left to right, to and fro, putting a little pressure on your backward stroke; work in the direction of the grain. Then, as it dries out, dust the chalk off the surface with a clean soft piece of rag which will bring your job to a fine finish. This weak mixture of water and acid kills off all the linseed oil and gives a rich finish. Some polishers do this with the use of a new piece of chamois leather instead of the palm of the hand, but I prefer the hand use.

After the final burnishing is completed with Vienna Chalk most old French Polishers use Ox-gall. This can be obtained from a butcher's slaughterman; although I don't think the amateur would venture into this. However, as a substitute Belco Liquid Polish can be used as a further burnishing.

BLEACHING

Before you proceed to bleach, check the job all over for finger marks or glue marks as these would show up, and they also resist the bleach. However, before bleaching prepare yourself with a pair of rubber gloves and protective eye glasses, with two grass brushes and a mask to be on the safe side. Bleaching procedure is applied with No. 1 and No.2 Chemical Solution. Apply No. 1 bleach first (shake up before using). Brush in well with the special grass brushes. Separate brushes must be used for each solution, and great care must be taken to see that they do not become mixed up. Allow about five minutes for No. 1 bleach to soak in; or just before it dries off, apply No. 2 bleach solution with the second grass brush (keep them separate). Apply with even strokes going along with the grain. This process may be repeated if required. Wash off any chemical residue with warm water, or Methylated Spirit when dry. Then, paper down with fine sandpaper and dust off — giving 24 hours drying time before waxing or polishing.

Oxalic acid may be used for cheapness — mixed with hot water. But this has certain definite limitations, because of its tendency to turn certain woods and veneers slightly red. If the correct procedure is taken, the bleached job will stand up well. Also, when bleaching use non-metallic containers only; and if the bleach comes in contact with the skin, wash off immediately with water. The well-known woods such as Walnut, Mahogany and Oak, all bleach well; but they will require two applications of solution. Other woods such as Rosewood, Ebony, Satinwood and Cherry are difficult, or cannot be bleached. Beech, Elm or Ash, bleach easily.

STOPPING AND BRUISES

Another way to get rid of a bruise, is to dig it with a penknife — making small pin holes, and refill them with coloured wax to match your job; then paper off the surplus wax. If the bruise is not too deep, you can take it out with a hot iron and a damp rag, by placing the damp rag over the bruise, then rubbing it, and finally iron over it.

There are various types of Stoppings which can either be bought from DIY shops or you can make your own. Beaumontage stopping is a mixture of equal parts of Beeswax, crush resin, and two flakes of shellac. It is heated up in a square, flat tin. When it sets hard you can use it like sealing wax, rolling it in the palms of your hands. To use it, heat at the end of the stick with an electric soldering iron, and hold the stopping over the hole so that it runs onto the hole. If it is a deep hole repeat the process so that it is completely filled up. Allow it to dry hard, then level off with a wet chisel so that the surface is not scratched. For light woods, a good stopping can be made up from dried whiting mixed with white polish which we call Polisher's Putty. It can be worked into the holes with a penknife as it dries in about half an hour, and can be levelled off with a chisel; then glass-papered down. One advantage of this stopping, is that Spirit Stain will take over it. But before applying the stopping, put a few drops of polish into the holes. Another cheap, home-made stopping for unimportant work such as shelves and fitments, can be made up from Plaster of Paris and glue size, as it sets fairly quickly. But, as a craftsman, I prefer to buy all my materials from the polishing manufacturers, as you can then be sure of first-class quality. Also, you can buy various colours of stopping and hard wax to match your job of Mahogany, Teak, Walnut, Rosewood, etc.

Therefore, the beauty of these hard coloured waxes for stopping up holes is that there is no need to colour them up, as in most cases they match the job.

COLOURING

To be a professional French Polisher you must have the correct materials, which can only be purchased from the polishing manufacturers. I am sure they would be only too pleased to send on a price catalogue, as it is essential to have the correct powders and stains to make up colours of your choice.

Spirit Colour

When matching up colours, it is often found that there is that particular cast that cannot be obtained by mixing black and red. Therefore, one has to use spirit colours. To obtain a Mahogany colour we use a small amount of Sanders' Red Polish, a small amount of Black Polish, ½ teaspoonful of Brown Umber, and a teaspoonful of Spirit Yellow. All of these colours are added to ¼ pint of polish and Methylated Spirit mix (two thirds of polish, one third of spirit), then adjust your colour of your choice. Dip your pencil brush into the colour. Try it on the back of sandpaper, or the back of your hand. A great deal of judgement is required to mix the correct colour.

Walnut Colour

If you only require a small amount of colour, just mix two thirds of polish, to one third Methylated Spirit; this is about the right mixture of any liquid quantity. As for your Walnut colour, just add Burnt Sienna, Spirit Brown powder, a small amount of Vegetable Black or Gas Black; then a pinch of all these powders to adjust your colour accordingly.

I find that if you mix up your colour separately you can choose your colours at a glance. Obtain about six small ½ pint size clear bottles. Fill them up with two thirds of polish, one third Methylated Spirit, then add your powders; a teaspoonful of Bismark Brown (Mahogany) in one bottle, Spirit Yellow, Spirit Black, Spirit Green, Spirit Blue, Spirit Brown all in separate bottles. Now with this selection you can experiment on these colours. Spirit Green helps to shade down the red. Spirit Yellow tones down the red to more of an orange shade. Spirit Blue also tones down red. This can also be used on Walnut — if too fierce; use yellow or green on the sparing side as they are very strong powders.

Spirit Mauve

This is very useful in taking the greenish cast out from certain types of Walnut, but it must be applied before any other colours — this is essential, but it must be used weak.

Solid Orange Colours

These are also in powder form, but mostly used in painting out bruises and discoloured streaks on polished surfaces. To use these colours weak, mix with polish a small amount of Methylated Spirit, paint out with a small pencil brush, but with a larger brush on plywood edges. They are cheap solid powder colours such as Burnt or Brown Umber, Yellow Ochre, Yellow Chrome, Orange Chrome, Red Lead, Rose Pink, Vandyke Brown, Flake White, all of which can be very useful. The best method is to pour some polish and spirit into an egg cup (half and half), then dip your pencil brush into the polish and spirit. Dip the tip of your brush into the powders required and mix up on the back of glass-paper. Mix your colours like an artist with his pallet — a bit of this and that. It is a good way of gaining colour experience as practice makes perfection. When polishing Walnut, a good tip is to put some Yellow Ochre into ½ pint of polish and fad up, not too strong. This will tone Walnut up if on the dark side. When painting plywood edges, mix up on the *thick side* like paste so as to blind the edges out. Paint once round, let it dry, then repeat if required. Paper down when dry, dust down and fad up with a dip of linseed oil on your fad, not too much oil; then finish edges when polishing the top of table with a rubber.

Fiddle Back Mahogany

This is very difficult to colour especially when quartered. Therefore, great care should be taken, but before staining, wash down with warm water to raise the grain and sand down when dry. Stain with Bichromate of Potash and when dry, paper down lightly. Should the job require a darker shade, stain on top of the Bichromate with Mahogany oil stain, as this will eliminate a lot of drying time; but try to obtain your colour by staining instead of colouring, as this will save a lot of headaches. Therefore, if the individual desires to colour up, standing in front of the job so as to view it at the side angle, will result in change of a different colour, as it will look dark at one angle and light on the opposite. Fiddle Back Mahogany is very unpredictable on colour.

EBONISING

Most polishers dislike ebonising. There is no beauty in the colour

c

— it is jet black. However, this can be made up by yourself with Black Spirit Powder or Gas Black. Dissolve the black powder in white polish, approximately a tablespoonful to a pint of white polish. Clean up the job thoroughly before staining. To mix your own stain, add spirit black powder (about a tablespoonful) to dissolve into ½ pint Methylated Spirit with a dash of polish (a small egg-cupful). Shake up well and stain with a pad of cotton wool or soft rag. Coat the stain with polish to seal it and lightly paper down when dry. As there is no colouring to proceed with just carry on fadding up with black polish and finish off with the rubber as the intense black will build itself up. It is possible to purchase the Black Ebony polish already made up from the manufacturers.

If the job requires filling in, Plaster of Paris can be used to obtain a full grain, but mix Lamp Black or Spirit Black with the plaster as this will kill the white when it dries. (See notes on the use of Plaster of Paris).

Some woods are more suitable than others, although Cherry, Pear, Holly, Apple and Sycamore are excellent for ebonising. When the ebonising is completed it will have a high gloss. However, some polishers use the dulling procedure to make an eggshell finish with the finest pumice or rotten-stone powder by brushing on with these powders. Some polishers prefer to wire down the surface with very fine wire wool No. (0000) or (000). But dust off first, and apply some turps on a rag; wipe the surplus off, then wire down again with No. (0000) fine wire wool, and dust off.

GENERAL HINTS

Water Staining

It is very important before staining to always wash down the job with warm or hot water. This will raise the grain so that the wood can be papered down nice and smoothly when dry. Now apply the water stain. Allow 12-24 hours to dry, and seal it with two coats of white polish or coloured polish.

Reviver

This is a cleaning mixture of several ingredients. An old polisher's recipe to clean up antiques and old furniture, is lemon oil mixed with powder pumice or rotten-stone; then rub down and clean off with a soft cloth. A cheap reviver can be made up with 1 part vinegar, 1 part Linseed Oil and 1 part Methylated Spirit.

Scratches

Scratches can sometimes be removed by painting in with Iodine on Mahogany with a small pencil brush.

Wax Finish

Wax finish that has been damaged with water or spirits can easily be restored. First clean off all the dirt, and with a saturated cloth of Turpentine wash down well. Also clean with a good reviver. The wax polish can be made up with 4oz. of raw Linseed Oil, 4oz. of Beeswax mixed up to a paste. Then add 1 quart of Turpentine and mix thoroughly. Repolish with a soft cloth, allow to dry, and burnish up with a fresh piece of soft cloth.

To Remove Dark Patches

These may be removed by bleaching them with a solution of Oxalic Acid. Mix up 2oz. of Oxalic Crystals to 1 pint of hot water or Methylated Spirit. Apply this with a small brush onto the dark patch and leave it for 10 minutes. Several applications may be required to remove it. Wash off with a weak solution of ammonia (mix 1 tablespoonful to a quart of warm water).

Oil Pigment Colour Stain

This is a quick method to shade Walnut, Mahogany and Oak. It is used as a weak stain — solid pigment powders, mixed with Linseed Oil. The mixture is 4oz. of any colour pigment with 1 part of Turpentine, Naphtha or Benzene, to equal parts of boiled or raw Linseed Oil; then applied with a rag or wadding, and wiped off. Always test your stain on a piece of the same wood. All stains should be applied evenly on all surfaces. Some polishers prefer to brush on the stain, others use wadding or rag. Pigment oil stains should be stirred well and strained through a piece of muslin. I would not advise this stain on good class work as it fades, but it is a cheap and quick method for amateur work.

Stains

A good point to note on staining, is to always make up more stain than you actually need; especially with a big job, as it is disastrous to run out whilst on a job and not have sufficient to complete the process. Even with experience, it is impossible to obtain the exact match to mix up fresh stain.

Blooming

A white and grey casting on polish, laquer and varnish surfaces usually caused by dampness or a drop in temperature. This is sometimes called 'chilling' in the trade. To overcome this, my advice and experience is to apply a hair dryer over the surface from left to right until the bloom disappears, but give the surface time to dry off first.

Precaution: When mixing acid and water, always remember to pour the acid into the water and never pour water onto the acid. Always wear protective clothing such as rubber gloves, eye shields, etc.

Rag On The Rubber

This is a very important item. Keep the rag free from grit and grease, as the amateur may tend to use too much Linseed Oil. Therefore, wash out the rag in Methylated Spirit or change it. Always pull back the rag when charging the rubber with polish.

STRIPPING

It is essential to use stripper that is spirit based, because water based strippers removes the unwanted finish. The washing down process on bare wood may raise the grain, and will become soft and feel slightly fluffy — especially on soft woods — then again it will lose its hard smooth surface. It is not advisable to use water based stripper.

When purchasing commercial strippers, it will inform you in the directions for use, whether the contents are water or spirit based. If directed to wash down with water, then it is water based; and if it is involving the use of Methylated Spirit, it is a spirit based stripper. Therefore, it is advisable to read the directions thoroughly.

There is an art in stripping. If the surface of old polish is not cleaned off properly, it leaves patches and shows up when polished. There are several good strippers on the market, but the one I have always used and recommended is the Jaxastryp, manufactured by

Sonneborn & Rieck Ltd. (address at back of book). However, this Jaxastryp stripper is ideal for polish work and it will not interfere with the colouring of the job. It can also be used for paint and cellulose. Before using this stripper use a pair of rubber gloves and protective glasses. Pour it into a strong tin, as it is a chemical stripper. Proceed to dip your brush into the stripper and apply all over your job. If it is a chest, take the drawers out and brass handles off, this will make a nice clean job of it. Now proceed in wetting the job all over. Start on the sides of the chest, then front rails and the top last. Leave the stripper on for 15 minutes or more and you will see the stripper action taking place as small bubbles will appear on the surface. Then strip off with a 2″ paint scraper. It is possible you may have to apply the stripper two or three times before all of the polish comes off completely, as it depends on the thickness of the old polish. But after your job has been stripped, it must be washed down with Methylated Spirit with a rag or clean, soft brush. This we call in the trade, neutralizing. Then wipe off the Methylated Spirit with a soft, clean piece of rag, the spirit dries very quickly.

There is another method in stripping old furniture when the old polish only needs the top layers to come off without a complete strip — see instruction listed under antiques — which we call 'doctoring' or 'first aid'.

When you have completed the stripping process and washed down with Methylated Spirit (neutralized), let it dry for about 10 minutes then smooth down with fine glass-paper. Dust down — you are then ready to stain — (if required) — fill in, fad up, colour, finish off etc., in stages.

In cases of a newer job where the polish may not be obscured by layers of dirt or wax and does not want to be stripped; only the top surface to be cleaned off; then I would advise to use just Turps and Linseed Oil (half and half). Apply it on a soft piece of rag and rub it in well, then finish off with a clean piece of rag. A good tip is to finish off with a small quantity of vinegar on a damp piece of rag and rub dry.

With regard to stripping, I would not advise one to use caustic soda or similar materials to remove polish as it is possible to darken woods such as Oak or Mahogany. However, if dark woods do not matter to you, you can make up your own stripper by using ½ lb of rock ammonia with ½lb of crude soap, or, 1lb of washing soda with 1 gallon of hot water. Apply it with a hard scrubbing brush, brushing in hard, then wash off with clean warm water and neutralize with vinegar. The water will raise the grain. When dry, paper down with medium glass-paper and dust off. Turned legs and moulds are frequently stripped by continually brushing the liquid stripper constantly wet until the polish softens up, then strip off with No. 3 wire wool. Then neutralize with Methylated Spirit and clean up again with fine wire wool No. 000 until it is nice and smooth. Then lightly paper down with fine flour paper, and dust down with soft rag.

OLD FURNITURE, REPAIRED AND POLISHED

On purchasing an old chest or a piece of furniture, it is likely you will have to restore it. For example, take an old chest. One may have to replace pieces of veneer that are missing; the rails may need patching up here and there; or a foot may need replacing — a polisher has to weigh up the pros and cons of the job, and judge the correct procedure to repair it. If it is not an antique or a valuable piece of furniture, firstly, I would advise to strip it with a chemical stripper or mix up a reviver — one third of Turps, Linseed Oil and Methylated Spirits. If only a clean up is required then paper down with No. 1 glass-paper, then repeat with fine flour paper and wipe off. Now that the chest has been stripped or cleaned up and the repair work completed, the bare parts are ready for matching up in colouring, so now one has to choose which stain to use. Walnut crystals can be used on Walnut jobs; when dry, seal it with two or three coats of Button Polish as this will give a fine golden colour on the brown Walnut background.

Therefore, you may have a Mahogany job. With this you stain with Bichromate of Potash. To attain a dark, deep Mahogany colour mix some Walnut crystals (about half and half). This can be diluted with water to attain a weaker colour as these are both water stains. For filling, paste filler can be used or Plaster of Paris. Add Rose Pink powder for Mahogany and add Vandyke Brown powder for Walnut. When the filler is dry, give two coats of polish to seal it. Also, with Plaster of Paris, oil as usual with Linseed Oil, then wipe and paper off.

The next procedure is to colour down the new repair work to match up to the original colour. But before this, after papering the job until it is nice and smooth, you must work up a thin surface of polish with a rubber, with just a touch of Linseed Oil to work the polish in. The next step is to make up a small amount of colour, using half polish and half Methylated Spirits and adding some Spirit Black, Bismark Brown powder, and a touch of Spirit Yellow; and mix up well.

In colouring up, always try out your colour on the back of your hand, or on the back of sandpaper. This colouring procedure is where most skill and experience comes into play — in making up the correct colour. Apply the colour with a pencil brush, a No. 5 or 6 camel hair brush, and tone down the light parts to match the original colour; but extra care must be taken to have plenty of light facing the job. Stand back and view your colouring before applying more colour. When dry, fix your colour with two coats of polish. Apply with a rubber lightly, then proceed with your polishing. To attain a nice, clean job, take off all the handles and remove all drawers. Repair work requires a great amount of skill and judgement applied to the job. An amateur may attain a certain amount of cabinet-making experience which is an interesting and rewarding job. Once you have accomplished a repair job to your satisfaction, it makes one feel very proud.

TYPES OF POLISH

It is advisable to attain the knowledge of these various coloured polishes as it will help the amateur immensely. For example: After staining Mahogany with Bichromate Stain, it is fadded with *Garnet Polish*. This will tone the Mahogany and give a warmer and deep brownish tone. Button Polish should not be used on Mahogany as it tends to give the wood a cloudy yellowish appearance. Although *Button Polish* is used to fad up on Walnut — it should be used very sparingly, otherwise the Walnut will become too yellowish.

White Polish

This is mostly used on bleached or natural jobs and finished with transparent polish which is colourless. Garnet, Button, White are all polishes that are important for toning various types of timbers. Experience is the only way you can master these polishes, but experiment with these polishes and with various coloured powders, and the amateur will find it very interesting.

With regard to transparent polish, this is mostly used on the finishing process as it is colourless. My advice is do not buy your polishes in a DIY shop because it is poor quality and sometimes oil or varnish is mixed with it, so avoid it. Buy the good quality polishes, stains, colours from the polish manufacturers (address at back of book). This is where I purchase from and the quality is guaranteed.

VARNISHING AND TYPES OF VARNISH

Varnishes can give you a very deep, high shine, with practice, and a little know-how. There are three classes of varnish; *Oil Varnish, Water Varnish,* and *Spirit Varnish.* I prefer to use the latter as it is quicker and easier to use. Spirit Varnish is ideal to use on doors, but they must be taken off their hinges and laid down flat as the varnish is floated on and not brushed in. With this method, a polisher's rubber can be used and time is not wasted on drying between coats of varnish. Spirit Varnish is the best to use of the three varnishes.

With varnish there is very little skill attached — only some experience required — so to varnish a door my method is quick and easy. The first step is to stain the door to your required colour with oil stain or spirit stain. It should be applied quickly and wiped off quickly. Stain sections of the door individually. When complete it only takes 15 minutes to dry with spirit stain. When the stain is dry apply two coats of polish, either with a fad or rubber. Wait until your first coat of polish is dry before applying the second coat. Then, rub down lightly with a piece of worn flour paper, slightly oiled. Make up a mixture of **polish, varnish and Methylated Spirits, say one third of each in a** pint bottle, and shake up well before using. Apply the mixture onto your rubber, then smear a little Linseed Oil on the surface of the rubber to start off with. Work the oil out with the rubber so that no oil is left in the job, and work with the grain in long strokes. Now the door should have a nice thin shine. Give the polish time to dry (about 15 minutes). Whilst waiting, get your new brush ready — a soft 2″ or 3″ brush.

Now lightly brush on the White Hard Varnish, in fact float it on. This is where experience comes into play as the brush must not be too wet otherwise you will get runnings. As the varnish has been applied to the door, allow drying time of about 20 minutes, then dip up with the new rubber. The rag is also very important. It must be of an open grain material. Apply the mixture fairly wet on the rubber, lightly tap the rubber on the back of sandpaper and lightly **apply the polish onto the surface of varnish,** *No oil is to be used.* Now with the rubber you can take out any brush marks that are left on the job. Charge your rubber two or three times to attain a nice body on the door. If a deeper shine is required allow one or two hours to dry, and paper down with an oily, old piece of flour paper; then wipe the oil off and repeat the process.

White Hard Varnish is recommended for polishing with rubber, as this varnish gives a very high degree of protection. But it must be of good quality, as it has a good resistance to wear and tear. It is ideal for table-tops subjected to heavy usages. For table-tops, always strip off the old polish before applying the spirit varnish or it is liable to crack up. Use the same procedure as mentioned previously for varnishing the door. With this process, room temperature is an important factor for varnishing. Between 70-80 degrees Fahrenheit is advisable. A well ventilated room is also advisable and very important, as it will allow the varnish to dry rapidly and harden. Dust can often spoil beautiful workmanship by settling on the surface, so keep the dust down by sprinkling the floor with water, or better still with wet sawdust.

ADVICE AND DEFECTS

Bare Wood

Clean up well. Use No. 1½ sandpaper and finish on No. 0. Dust down.

Staining

On using water stain always wash down with warm water. Allow 2 or 3 hours drying time. This wash down raises the grain and allows the job to be papered down smoothly. Use No. 1½ sandpaper and finish on No. 1 — No. 0.

Oil Stains

Allow 2 or 3 hours drying time.

Spirit Stain

Add a small quantity of polish with spirit stain to hold colour. Allow 15 minutes drying time, then seal it with two coats of polish. Allow time between coating.

Filling In

When filling in with Plaster of Paris allow a good 2 hours drying time. Use only raw Linseed Oil to kill the white — mix coloured powder with the plaster, according to the required colour of wood.

Scratches

This can be overcome if they are only slight scratches by rubbing Linseed Oil on with a piece of soft rag or by your finger. If the scratches are deep, then fill in with coloured wax and lightly remove excess with a penknife. Recolour if necessary.

Finger Marks

This may be due to using excessive oil, and with it being greasy, it may not have been worked out properly. Therefore, it is best to paper down and repolish, using a spirit finish at the end.

Wine Glass Marks

These white wine marks can be removed by rubbing lightly with fine wire wool (No. 000), or with an old worn oily piece of flour paper (fine). Then wipe clean with soft rag, recolour with a pencil brush and allow ten minutes to dry. Then give it two coats of polish. Allow to dry and repolish. Sometimes you may remove the marks with Methylated Spirit on a piece of rag, but not too wet. Rub the spirit on the white marks until it fades out. Rebuild up after recolouring; then repolish the surface.

Water Marks

These are sometimes caused by plants being over-watered and left to lay on a polished surface. There are several ways to overcome this. First of all wipe dry the water. Then wipe over the water mark with Camphorated Oil, rubbing well into the surface several times, then apply Vinegar on a soft rag to remove the oil. Polish the area with Brasso as if you are polishing metal, but do not let the Brasso dry white. Wipe clean, then wax over. In cases where the water has been left too long, wipe dry, then apply a warm rag and rub in well. Then paper down the white water mark with a fine piece of oily worn flour paper. Dust off, and apply two coats of polish. Allow to dry, recolour if necessary with a pencil brush and repolish the surface.

Ink Stains

To remove these stains, apply a weak solution of Oxalic Acid or Nitric Acid with a brush, rub in well and allow to dry. This may dry white, then rub in Camphorated Oil, and wipe dry. **An alternative** method is to paper out the ink mark or lightly scrape out the mark, then fill in with coloured wax, recolour, seal it with polish, lightly paper down with old worn flour paper and repolish.

White Heat Marks

These are sometimes caused by hot plates placed on a polished surface. These can be removed by one of several alternatives. If the heat marks are deep use the Methylated Spirit treatment; wet the marked area with spirit on a piece of rag then set alight the Methylated Spirit. Let if burn out first before repeating the process. But, be careful, as too much spirit can damage the whole surface. Then, lightly paper down, rebuild up the whole area with a polish rubber and recolour. Now repolish the whole area.

Alternatively, **one can use a mixture of Linseed Oil and Turps of** equal amounts. Rub in well with a piece of rag or apply it with a brush and allow the mixture to remain on the white marks for ten minutes or more. Then wipe off and apply a film of Vinegar over the whole area. Camphorated Oil can also be used by rubbing in and wiping off; then applying a film of Vinegar over the surface. This must be repeated several times.

Fading Colour

This can be caused by being exposed to the sun or through dampness, and can only be overcome by stripping the faded area. Try first to paper down, recolour and repolish before stripping; although if the sun has taken off the polish with the colour, it is advisable to strip and start from the beginning.

Chilling

This is due to working in a damp workshop or room. The polished surface turns a greenish colour or slightly blue when polishing or stiffing off — when this happens stop polishing. Sometimes a polisher can overcome this by applying a hair dryer over the surface for about ten minutes to dry out the dampness. Alternatively, mix **Linseed Oil and Turpentine equally and rub in over the surface** when dry and wipe off. Apply a thin film of Vinegar afterwards and wipe off clean. In bad cases, paper down with fine flour paper slightly oiled with Linseed and repolished — this can be more effective.

Dullness On Polished Surfaces

If this happens after you have polished and finished the job, it will be due to using too much Linseed Oil. In other words, the polisher has buried the oil and not worked the oil out. However, to correct this the polisher must cut down the surface with fine flour paper. Wipe off, give the surface a couple of straight rubbers (no oil). Use **half and half polish and spirit, then finish off** spiriting out — this process will eliminate the oil.

Spiriting

The process in which you only use Methylated Spirit on the surface of the rubber to take out all the traces of oil.

Whips and Ropiness

This is caused when the rubber is too fully charged with polish. It pulls up the surface making it rough and causes lines and ridges. Stop polishing when this happens, allow the surface to dry. Cut down with an oily piece of fine flour paper and start afresh using only half the spirit and polish, and have the rubber only damp and not wet. Add some pressure on the rubber to flatten down.

Stopping

Polishers use this to fill in holes, small cracks and scratches, and can be obtained in several colours to suit the job from the polishing manufacturers.

Polisher's Rubber

This is used in the trade for finishing off. It is wadding (cotton wool) with a rag covering the wadding to give it a finer finish. The difference between a rubber and a fad is that rag is not used on a fad.

Oils

This is another important factor. White Mineral Oil is advocated to be used on bleached jobs, Sycamore, Maple, natural finishes, polished with white polish and finished with transparent polish. Linseed Oil is mostly used on Mahogany, Walnut and Oak. A good piece of advice is to mix the two oils together equally, but not on bleached jobs.

Water Stains

Before staining with water stains, always wash down the job with warm or hot water. This will raise the grain on the job. Paper down when dry. Therefore, when staining, the grain will not rise.

Woods

Where new woods are used, in some cases, planing comes into operation which sometimes leaves plane marks. To overcome this a scraper is used. A lot of preparation comes into play with new woods. Therefore, great care and judgement is necessary. Always check over the new wood carefully. Make sure there are no defects or bruises and that it is free from grease, finger and glue marks, or these will show up when polished. All of these defects can be removed by using a good piece of sandpaper, use No. 1½ and No. 1 glass-paper; then finish with fine flour paper as this should eliminate all minor imperfections so that the job is nicely prepared for polishing.

Wood With Machined Surfaces

With woods that have been machine planed, always damp down with hot water before papering down as the hot water will raise any ridges or defects, and papering down will eliminate all marks and will not show through when staining.

Polish Bottles

A craftsman or a good DIY man must be organised. Obtain three or four clear bottles, then fill up each individual bottle with White Polish in one, Garnet Polish in another, Button Polish in the third and special Pale Polish in the last. Label each bottle so that you will know from a glance what type of polish to use. A good tip to remember when using a bottle of polish is to cut a "V" shape in the side of the cork and place it into the top of the bottle. This is a great help when dipping up your fad or rubber as it allows the polish to flow evenly.

Grooved Cork

Polishes

These types of polishes you will get to know from experience as you go along. Garnet Polish is a dark brown colour. Button Polish is a yellowish golden colour, ideal for Walnut (to start off with); finishing the job off with Transparent Polish, which we call Extra Special Pale Polish (colourless). Use different polishes to start off with, as it depends on the colour required. To polish Sycamore use White Polish and finish off with Transparent Polish.

Rag And Wadding

Selecting these materials is a very important item, but to obtain the best quality it is advisable to purchase from polishing suppliers. Wadding is purchased from drapery shops — ask for unbleached wadding. Do not purchase it from a chemist, as it is medicated cotton wool — too starchy for polishing. Rag is very important. Select a fairly fine grain linen, not too open or too thick. Irish linen is very good, or worn pillow cases that have been well washed.

Colour Brushes

This is another important factor, as a good camel hair can give you a first-class job, and last for several years with care. But before using a new colour brush, soak it in polish for two days suspended in a jar. A cardboard lid is ideal on top of the jar, then push the top of the brush through the lid to suspend it, so that it is about one inch from the bottom of the jar. When brushes have been well soaked, squeeze out the surplus polish and bring the hair to a point between your fingers and put aside for a day or so. This will keep the brush in ideal condition, as when in use the hair will not come out. Soften in polish and not Methylated Spirit, otherwise it will wash out the setting polish around the roots of the hair. Colour brushes mostly used in the trade should be No. 5, 6 or 7 camel hair mop, quill bounded on a wooden handle. For very fine colouring use a small pencil brush, this ideal for the job. In colouring your job, to pick out the light shades, a good practice when dipping your brush into the colour is to squeeze the excess colour out between the side of your colour jar and finger, then wipe your brush on a piece of wadding to attain an even stroke when colouring. Also, stand back at arms length from the job, as this will give you a better view on picking out the colour.

ANTIQUE RESTORATION

I find it best to clean up the whole job then repair it afterwards, but some restorers work the opposite way. When your job is cleaned up to start with, I find it much easier to colour and match up to the original work. Therefore, if you have to repair a Regency cabinet of Burr Yew or Mahogany, and obtain the veneer to match up, there is very little to colour up. After the clean up process, and the repair parts have been completed, make sure all the glue marks are cleaned off. Then stain up the weak spirit stain — you can make this up yourself. Just make up a small amount. First, obtain a small, clean bottle and pour in ¼ pint of Methylated Spirit, add an egg-cupful of polish (just to hold the stain colour), then add about a teaspoonful of Spirit Mahogany Powder with just a pinch of Spirit Yellow just so that the Mahogany is not too red. Your stain is now made up, but first try it out on a piece of spare veneer or Mahogany wood. If too strong, dilute with spirit, then dab the stain on the repaired parts and wipe off almost as soon as it has been applied. Put the stain on with a clean piece of white rag. The stain dries in a matter of five minutes. Then, apply a coat of polish, and when dry add another coat of polish. Give this a good ten minutes to dry, then paper down lightly with flour paper and dust down ready to colour up with a small pencil brush if required.

REPRODUCTION OF ANTIQUE OAK

Oak reproduction can almost be the real old antique if given the correct procedure. Therefore, some of the tricks of the trade in distressing the job is carried out by rounding the corners with a file, making bruises with a piece of metal or a heavy bicycle chain, knocking the edges with a hard piece of wood, adding scratches here and there with a nail, and to add a more antique quality, a few ink marks are put in. Some old antique polishers have some tricks up their sleeves known only to themselves. With regard to staining, some polishers use Jacobean Oil to stain. When dry, it is shaded out by rubbing down lightly with fine wire wool (No. 000) starting in the middle of the panel and working outwards. This will give a rubbed effect, being light in the middle of the panel, and a darker shade around the edges, giving something of a picture frame effect. Also, you can stain with Vandyke Walnut Crystals (water stain). Put a dash of (.880) Ammonia to drive it into the grain and make it a deeper, dark colour. If you require a darker, warmer tone, go over it again with Walnut Oil Stain, but make sure your first coat of stain is thoroughly dry. *Note* that when using (.880) Ammonia, mix only a tablespoonful with stain as it is very strong. Use rubber gloves and protective glasses. Staining to colour depends on the period the job belongs to, as some antiques are maltreated according to its age, and this is a very wide subject to go into. However, with regard to mouldings, these can be stained dark, and when dry these can be papered lightly on top to give a light and dark effect. When staining with oil stain, give it two coats of French Polish to seal it, but allow the stain to dry thoroughly first.

OAK COLOURING AND STAINING

There are several proprietary stains such as Golden Oak, Medium Brown, Black Oak, Yellow Oak, Dark Oak and Fumed Oak, and these stains give the depth of colour. To attain a *Green Waxed Oak,* clean up the Oak and treat it with a spirit stain by dissolving spirit soluble (aniline green powder) in Methylated Spirit. Measure half a teaspoonful of the green powder into half a pint of Methylated Spirit, and add about an egg-cupful of French Polish; this helps to hold the stain in. Make up a good pad of cotton wool, or use soft rag, and apply stain quickly and evenly by straight strokes, as this spirit stain dries quickly, otherwise the job will be unsatisfactory and will tend to be patchy. Allow 15 minutes or more for drying time, then paper down lightly with fine glass-paper, sealing it with two coats of White Polish. Now this process is ready to fill the grain in with *White Wax Polish.* Rub the wax well into the grain with a soft piece of rag, as by rubbing vigorously you will work up a gloss. Then repeat the process by using more wax. If oil stains are used on Oak to attain a darker shade, allow the stain to dry then apply two coats of French Polish by rubber, before applying a wax finish, otherwise it may lift the stain and make the job patchy.

Filling In Oak

A good, cheap filler to use, is a handful of French Chalk to a pint of French Polish, either White or Garnet Polish according to the shade of colour required. Apply with a brush, and coat the work all over, stirring the mixture frequently to attain the correct mixture. Then allow it to dry and paper down with fine sandpaper and dust off. With this process you can polish it to give a satin smooth finish or wax it. For *Natural Oak* where staining is not required, just polish it, making sure your job is free from finger or glue marks otherwise it will show under the polish especially on natural work. It is very important to give it a good looking over and to give it a good papering down with No. 1 glass-paper and fine paper. Use only White Polish first on fadding up, then finish off with transparent Clear Polish with your rubber, but paper down after fadding up before using the rubber. *Polishing Carvings* using this process requires the polisher to use a stiff brush. When waxing carvings, apply the wax to the brush and not to the job, as it may choke up in the corners. Draw the brush across the carvings to even out the wax and rub in well, then use a soft piece of rag to burnish up the carvings. When waxing carvings in antique furniture the process is much the same, but do not scrub out the antique wax too vigorously, leave some of the Black Wax in corners and angles to give that antique appearance. A good piece of advice before waxing is to give the job a thin eggshell shine by a few rubbers of White Polish as this will help to keep out the dust and dirt. It also seals the grain as a lot of handling is liable to make the job become soiled. In sealing the job first, you can always renew the wax polish finish when the surface gets too dirty.

DOCTORING AND FIRST AID

This is, without doubt, the most challenging of skills and craftsmanship one can master in the art of repair and polishing. Old antiques are governed by the refined professional care and skill of French Polishing to enable it to be restored to its original state. Therefore, one has to judge and analyse the state of repair and to examine the best use of skill to approach the job. On very old antique furniture that may have been inherited, it is best not to strip it, as one will never be able to restore its original colour, which has been aged over the years, and has a mellow cast.

Therefore, one has to preserve the maximum state of its *original colour* as most old antiques have been misused, or not used, and perhaps stored in a damp attic for several years where it has accumulated dirt and grime. Where diseased or damaged parts are to be repaired it will probably mean that a careful search has to be made to obtain a piece of veneer or timber suitable to match the job. But it will be rewarding when the job is completed, and be adequate compensation for the time spent in search of the replacements, as most damaged veneers and timbers have to be spliced in with great care. It is essential not to strip it as explained, and therefore, I shall let you into a trade secret which we call 'Doctoring' or 'First Aid' (also known as the Amalgamation method), which means applying a new finish over an old one, mostly used in antique restoration where an old polished surface has cracked up or grime and dirt has to be disposed of in a cleaning up process.

It is best to work in a dry, heated room, or outside on a warm summer's day, otherwise the humid air may cause the finished work to cloud up. To start off, if you have a four or five drawer chest, take all the drawers out and handles off to attain a nice clean job, and you also have a nice clean sweep on the drawers. Good advice is to buy yourself a new 2″ paint brush, then you can be sure of a good finish. Also purchase some Cellulose Thinners and Methylated Spirit, and pour a cupful of Cellulose Thinners into a pint of Methylated Spirit. Shake up well, and pour some into a cup, or an open top vessel (not metal or plastic). Start with the drawers first. Tilt them up on their ends (at a 45 degree angle), dip your brush into the cup or vessel of liquid, holding your drawer in your left hand and slightly tilting it, then wet the surface and brush freely straight up and down on the surface as quickly as possible, using a swinging action lightly. Then brush dry with smooth, straight strokes, and you will find the cracks disappearing. Do the same on all drawers then repeat if required when dry.

Use the same method on your chest, but tilt the top of the chest at an angle. Wet up well with the brush, and apply with straight strokes keeping your brush moving all the time with quick actions — speed is essential, and is the art of the process. When completely dry (approx. half an hour) rub down with fine wire wool (000). Rub smoothly so that it is nice and flat and dust down. Now wax or polish it. For a lacquer finish, use *Cellulose Thinners only,* NOT *Methylated Spirit.*

This method is the next best to stripping.

SPIRIT AND SOLID COLOURS

Solid Coloured Powders

These powders can be of many uses: to mix with Plaster of Paris; to colour when filling in Mahogany, Walnut, Oak, etc.; to tone in with other colours mixed in polish and Methylated Spirit; and in water stain for shading.

Colours used include Red Lead, Rose Pink, Flake White, Yellow Ochre, Pink and Canary Litharge, Lithopone, Yellow and Orange Chrome, Gas Black, Lamp Black, Venetian Red, Brown Umber,

Raw Turkey, Burnt Umber, Titanium White, Burnt and Raw Sienna.

Spirit Colours

Mixed with polish and spirits in equal amounts:
Bismark Brown (Reddish Brown)
Chrysoidine (Yellowish Red)
Spirit Black — Spirit Yellow — Brunswick Green — Spirit Mauve — Spirit Blue and Green.

Crystal Colours

Bichromate of Potash, Green Copperas and Vandyke Crystals. These are to be mixed up with warm water. Add a dash of (.880) ammonia for penetration if required.

Wire Wool Grades

No. (0000), (000), (00)
No. (1), (2), (3), (4)
No. 3 and 4 are mostly used in stripping off.

LACQUERS AND SYNTHETICS

There are several types of lacquers and these can give a very artistic and attractive finish. The advantages of lacquers is that they can be sprayed on with considerable speed, and are resistant to water and spirit and also have rapid drying speed. Most furniture manufacturers use lacquer because it is quicker and cheaper, and is a modern development in polish finishing, but it looks very synthetic.

There are two methods for lacquer application: spray type, and hand brush for home-owners. Purchase a fine soft 3″ brush. Before applying the lacquer, make sure the groundwork has been nicely prepared. Fill in with a silex base type with a small amount of Linseed Oil and Japan dryer. This can be thinned with spirit, Naphtha or Turpentine of good quality. If the grain of wood is wide open, make the paste filler thicker. Mix up to your desired requirements — a putty knife is best to give a good mixing. Only use a small amount of thinning to start with, then add your solid colour powders to the required colour desired. Most polish manufacturers have these paste fillers made up in various colours to suit the polisher's requirements. There is a substitue for filling in if the grain of wood is not too open, that is to paper down between each coat. If required, use a non grain-raising stain before applying the filler, and seal with two coats of lacquer sealer.

Brush Lacquer

When the surfaces have dried, lightly sandpaper with every procedure — ready to brush lacquer. Use a 3″ brush but make sure that the sanding sealer lacquer coats are absolutely hard before applying the brush lacquer. Apply the lacquer heavily loaded on the brush. Do not rub the brush on the side of the tin as bubbles will form on the surface. Brush evenly and lightly. Start in the middle of the job and work towards the ends. Work rapidly in long strokes evenly with the grain. Let the lacquer level itself and do not brush over. Repeat the process if required but only after the first coat of lacquer has dried hard. Lightly paper down and dust off before applying the second coat.

TYPES OF LACQUER

Clear Gloss Lacquer dries with a gloss. It can be thinned with lacquer thinners. Allow 2-3 hours drying time between additional coats.

Clear Flat Lacquer

This dries flat and can be mixed with a small amount of gloss lacquer.

Buffing Lacquer

Mostly used for buffing to a high polish. A very hard lacquer — clear or coloured.

Shellac Mixing Lacquer

Clear lacquer most suitable to mix with Shellac Polish. Makes a good blend.

Bleaching Lacquer

Most suitable for natural and very light woods. A very thin water white lacquer.

Bronzing Lacquer

Clear. Used for mixing with bronze powders.

Bar Top Lacquer

Very hard and durable. Used for bars and table-tops.

Shading Lacquer

Transparent. Ideal for shading. Comes in several colours.

Lacquer Thinners

These are mostly classified as slow, medium, or fast drying by their evaporation; but care should be taken in using fast drying thinners because of *'Blooming'* and will sometimes cause orange peel effect. Slow drying thinners is mostly known as retarders to prevent blooming on the surface.

REVIVERS

This is the term used in the trade for a mixture solution to clean up a polished surface. This mixture can be made up at home by an amateur, although the recipes have been a closely guarded trade secret for many years because of its great value to the tradesman.

Several ingredients go into making this up. Several individual French Polishers use their own experience with their special ingredients, but a good piece of advice is do not use too much Raw Linseed Oil in the Reviver for if the polished surface has several minor cracks in it like a small spiders web, the oil is liable to seep through and darken the cracks. Reviver is a great help to the polisher as if you use the correct ingredients to remove the old dirt and grease off the polished surface it is almost as good as repolishing. It is essential in most cases with regard to antique work where there is only a thin shine required on a polished job, as antiques do not have a high shine. Therefore, Reviver is mostly used in antique restoration. Below are the ingredients used to make up Revivers:

(No. 1) 1 part of Methylated Spirit
      1 part of Vinegar
      1 part of Raw Linseed Oil

(No. 2) 4 parts of Raw Linseed Oil
     1 part of Terebine
     12 parts of Vinegar

(No. 3) ½ pint of Methylated Spirit
     ½ pint of Vinegar
     1oz. Raw Linseed Oil
     ½oz. Butter of Antimony
     1oz. of Camphor
     (dissolved in Meth. Spirit)

(No. 4) 1 cupful of Acetic Acid
     1 cupful of Methylated Spirit
     1 egg-cup of Linseed Oil (Raw)
     2 pints of warm water

CELLULOSE FINISHING

This finish cannot be used on a rubber in the same method as French Polish. Cellulose finish is mostly used in the manufacturing firms, as this treatment is a spray finish, and has frequently superseded French Polishing over the last fifty years or more.

Cellulose is of a plasticised chemical source. The spraying technique on wood veneers needs no filling process. The veneered furniture is just one or two coats of sealer, then papered down, one coat of lacquer recoloured, and two or three coats of lacquer, then the job is finished. However, sometimes, if it is to be of a high standard finish, then it is pulled over by a polisher with a special pullover process.

The cellulose finish does have advantages over French Polishing as it is heat and water resistant, and very economical to furniture manufacturers. It also requires less man hours and skill — a quicker process. However, an important disadvantage is that damaged surfaces cannot be restored in the same manner as French Polishing, and therefore it has to be completely stripped and started afresh. Also, it can be of great risk to careless handling, as it is inflammable.

TERMS USED IN FRENCH POLISHING

Fadding Up: This is the first stage in polishing. Polish is applied to the wadding (cotton wool) without rag. Fadding is the quickest way of filling in the grain with polish but some experience is required with this as Linseed Oil is also used.

Filling In: This process comes after staining and before polishing as the open grain in the wood is filled in with either manufactured ready-made filler of different colours to suit the job, or with Plaster of Paris, with various coloured powders to mix in as required.

Dipping Up Or Charging a Rubber: Both have the same meaning, it is just down to the polisher's choice of term. To dip up or charge a rubber means to remove the rag covering the rubber and shake a quantity of polish onto it. However, a fad has no rag to remove, so you dip up polish straight onto it.

To Kill: A term used in the trade to eliminate an unwanted colour. For example, a redness in Mahogany is killed off by using green, and green can be killed off by using a weak red colour. As spirit colours can eliminate each other, sometimes a polisher may use a weak spirit yellow, spirit green, spirit blue to kill, or tone down red.

Grinder: This is a polishing rubber with a little fine pumice powder spread beneath the rag to flatten the polished surface when bodying up. It also increases the pull on the rubber. It cannot be used to finish off a job — use a fresh rubber.

Cutting Down: It means papering down a polished surface to flatten and level off ready for the next process.

Dulling Down: To take the high shine off of a polished surface — to make a matt finish. Cut down with a very fine flour paper, or use fine pumice powder and apply with a fine, soft brush, or with a piece of soft velvet cloth. For dulling, apply Turpentine with a spot of Linseed Oil mixed on a piece of soft rag. Cover the surface with this. Sprinkle a small quantity of fine pumice or crocus powder, then brush the surface lightly with straight strokes. Allow 24 hours for the polish to dry before dulling down. Fine wire wool can also be used (No. 000).

TERMS AND MATERIALS

Acetic Acid: Used in furniture revivers. Also removes ink stain, and found in vinegar.

Acetates: Solvent for nitro-cellulose.

American Potash: Mostly used for weathering Oak. Will turn the wood a deep brown and darkens the figure.

Ammonia: Can be used for fuming Oak. Very useful when water staining, acts as a penetration, drives the stain into the grain, also slightly darkens the stained wood.

Aniline Dyes: Can be purchased in various colours such as Black, Brown, Blue, Bismark Brown, Green, Red, Yellow, Purple, Maroon, Orange and Crimson. These dyes are used for making coloured stains, mixed with either water, oil or Methylated Spirit and polish for colouring.

Ageing: A time blending process, applied to varnish and oils in storage.

Alligatoring: A form of spider wed cracks. Appears on the top surface of a polished finish, caused by the underlying surface remaining relatively soft by not allowing the under surface to dry thoroughly.

Antique Finish: A polished finish on old furniture to give the appearance of age and greater wear.

Asphaltum: This is of a natural bitumen or asphalt. Mostly used for making a dark brown stain, mixed in turpentine. Solid form of broken bitumen pieces.

Benzine: A light gravity of petroleum distillate.

Beaumontage: A solid stick of shellac form, in a variety of colours, used for filling in deep cracks and imperfections on woods.

Benzolene: This is a more powerful solvent than Benzine. It is a coal tar naphtha and can be used to remove excessive oil when varnishing.

Bloom: A white and grey casting appears on top surfaces of lacquer, varnished and shellac finishes; sometimes called 'chilling' and is usually caused by dampness; moisture in the air; drop in temperature; too much Methylated Spirit in the rubber (polishing); cold humidity trapped under the underlying surface.

Bismark Brown: This is an aniline dye powder of strong, fierce red colouring. Be cautious when mixing. A red colour polish can be made up from this powder, made up with polish and Methylated Spirit in equal amounts.

Bichromate Of Potash: This is a crystal form, mostly used for making Mahogany stain and can also be used with Walnut stain and Oak. Gives a deep orange shade. Very strong crystals.

Bleach: A two process A and B chemical solution used to lighten the colour of woods and veneers.

Bleaching Lacquer: This has no bleach action, only used to prevent the woods from being darkened by filler. Use as a sealing lacquer.

Bleeding: Sometimes occurs in oil and spirit stains.

Brush Lacquer: Only used for brush application. Can be purchased clear or coloured, a lacquer solution.

Brown Umber: A brown solid pigment powder, sometimes used for shading, can be mixed with other solid powders.

Butter Of Antimony: This is a dark brown liquid sometimes used as an ingredient with furniture reviver. It also has a hardening effect.

Brunswick Black: A thick, black liquid, ideal for using as a floor stain, thinned down with turpentine it gives a slight shine when dried.

Brunswick Green: This is of a solid powder used mostly for killing red colour. Also used in mixing with other colour powders.

Catalyst Finish: A hard, tough finish ideal for bar counters, table-tops etc., has a rapid chemical reaction and a hard finish to withstand rough treatment. Resistant to water and spirit marks.

China Clay: Mostly used as wood filler paste.

Colour In Oil: This a pigment colour, ground and mixed with boiled or raw Linseed Oil. Ideal for shading.

Copal: Fossilized gum resin used to make an oil based varnish. Hardest natural resin. Comes from Africa and is a pale yellowish colour.

Copperas: A crystal form, dissolved in water, gives a muddy greenish colour. Used mostly to kill the redness in Mahogany. There are three kinds of Copperas a polisher uses: Blue Copperas, Green Copperas and White Copperas.

Crocus Powder: A very fine abrasive powder used in dulling a polished finish to give an eggshell appearance.

Camphor: Can be used in some furniture reviver.

Camphorated Oil: Very useful for the removal of water and heat marks on polished surfaces. Also used for medical purposes. Obtained from Asian Laurel wood tree.

Flake White: Polishers sometimes use this white powder, mixed in White Polish, to lighten the tone of wood.

French Chalk: A fine, white powder which can be used to make a thin paste filler.

Gas Black: A powder used to mix in with Plaster of Paris filler on an ebony finish. Sometimes a polisher mixes this in his colour.

Gold Size: A quick drying varnish used on gold paint and gold leaf, also useful to bind colours ground in turpentine.

Glue Size: Very useful to use with water stains, to mix in stains. Acts as a good binder.

Grain Raising: Roughness of wood caused by water stains or other materials. This can be eliminated by applying hot or warm water to raise the grain, then paper down when dry.

Hydrogen Peroxide: This is used for bleaching, one part to two parts of water to dilute.

Lamp Black: A black solid powder sometimes used for water coating, but only used on cheap jobs. Can also be used in ebonising and for Black waxing. Very useful in antique restoration, to make furniture look old.

Lacquer: This material has a fast drying finish. It contains a certain amount of nitro-cellulose in combination with various resins, gums and solvents.

Linseed Oil: A vegetable oil pressed out from the seeds of the flax plant. Can be obtained in either boiled or raw form, the latter is used in French Polishing as a lubricant.

Methylated Spirit: A solvent for polish and paint. Manufacturers use this for making French Polish and stains. Also used for mixing colours with polish. Can be purchased from DIY and oil shops.

Mineral Spirits: The same as White Spirit, used as a solvent for varnish, paints and enamels.

Mineral Oil: This is a fine, white oil used as a lubricant for rubber work when French Polishing.

Naphtha: Flammable, volatile liquid made by distilling petroleum coal tar, used as a cleaner or solvent for varnishes, paints and enamels.

Nitro-cellulose: A substance produced by the action of Nitric Acid. Raw cotton cellulose mixed with nitric — a base for lacquers. Also used in making explosive plastics.

Nitric Acid: Useful to remove ink stains. Colourless, corrosive acid — a chemical, sometimes mixed with stains.

Orange Peel: Similar to the skin of an orange, a bad lacquer finish, caused by too rapid drying of the lacquer.

Oxalic Acid: Can be used for a quick, cheap bleaching. Ideal to remove ink marks. Care should be taken when using this as it is classed as poison.

Oil Solubles: These are capable of being dissolved in Linseed Oil, Benzolene, Turpentine and Naphtha. Stains of this type sometimes called Red Oil, Yellow Oil.

Oil of Vitriol: The same as Sulphuric Acid.

Paste Filler: Refers to a filler for wood, a filling paste — material diluted with turpentine, naphtha, etc.

Paraffin, Medicinal: Sometimes used as a lubricant with a rubber in French Polishing on bleached and light woods. Sometimes mixed with Hydrocarbons.

Permanganate Of Potash: A salt of permanganic acid in a fine, crystal form. Can be used for stain making and produces a purple and a deep rich brown tone.

Plaster Of Paris: Used as a strong excellent wood filler. Superfine grade is best. Easy to obtain in oil shops.

Plasticizer: Material substance added to lacquer to increase toughness and flexibility of the nitro-cellulose process.

Pinholes: A massive formation of pinholes in a film of polish or lacquer during spraying application, sometimes due to air or gas bubbles forming on the surface. Rapid spraying can also cause this.

Pearl Ash: Some polishers still use this for stripping off old polish or varnish.

Poppy Oil: Used by some polishers in the old days as a lubricant in French Polishing. Preferable to Linseed Oil or White Oil.

Pigment Powders: Sometimes added to polish or lacquer to obtain a mild shading coloured product.

Precipitated Chalk: Used as a substitute for Vienna Chalk in the acid finish within the pounce bag.

Pullover: A procedure where a polisher pulls over the lacquered finish with a rubber charged with Cellulose to obtain a very high bright lustre finish.

Pumice Powder: A white, natural stone powder, which is pulverized to obtain a fine, soft abrasive — sometimes used in a polisher's rubber for rubbing down polished surfaces. The very fine grade is used.

Retarders: This is a slow drying solvent, added and mixed in lacquer to retard the drying time.

Resin: A solid substance, mostly used in Cellulose; resin and gums are used in making finishing materials. Gives toughness and increases adhesion.

Rose Pink: A solid, coloured powder very useful to mix with

Plaster of Paris which helps to kill the white. Mostly used on Mahogany woods.

Rotten-stone: Another fine abrasive. Has a fine cutting action, also a good polisher. The English and Belgian grades are advocated for furniture rubbing — much finer than pumice powder. Can also be used as a pounce bag.

Shellac: Mostly used for making French Polish.

Silex: A white powder substance. Can be used for making a thin paste filler, mixed with coloured powders. Also, non-shrinking powder when combined with oil.

Steel Wool: Very useful product. Fine wire wool (No. 000) can be used for dulling finished surfaces with wax or fine abrasive, No. 3, 2, 1, grades used for stripping polish or varnished surfaces.

Tack Rag: This is a piece of butter muslin that has been dipped in thin varnish, then wrung out and kept moist in an airtight tin so as to remain tacky. Used to wipe over surfaces, to pick up dust — very useful.

Turpentine: A colourless liquid volatile oil distilled, pure American turpentine is best (if obtainable), used to thin down chemical filler. Also used for making oil stains and wax polish.

Thinners: Mostly used to blend with lacquer solvent.

Tint: A term used to slightly colour wood with colour pigment powders or polish colours.

Touch-Up: A method where a polisher repairs damaged colour parts of furniture, to touch up a colour that is to blend in the colour to match up with the original.

Terebine: Sometimes used with a polish reviver, a drying agent. Also in varnish work to correct bad faults.

Vandyke Brown: A brown powder substance which can be used for stain making and for water coating, but ammonia must be added with glue size as a binder — use warm water.

Vandyke Crystals: In crystal form only. Ideal for making Walnut stain as known in the trade as walnut crystals — mixed up with warm water and a touch of ammonia added to it gives a deep brown colour — much better than the wash stain.

Volatile: Easily evaporated — a solvent that dries by evaporation.

Venetian Red: A powder form, added to Plaster of Paris to kill the white and produce a reddish tone.

Vienna Chalk: A precipitated chalk. White and soft, used in a pounce bag, with the sulphuric acid finish.

Vinegar: A sour liquid containing acetic acid and used in furniture reviver. Helps to kill the grease and oil.

Water White: A term used for transparent, colourless.

White Spirit: A pretroleum distillate, used as a substitute for turpentine. Also used to dilute in paint and for making some oil stains. Good for cleaning.

White Mineral Oil: This oil is less greasy than linseed oil. Use as a lubricant, the same as linseed oil — just a matter of choice when French Polishing — I prefer it mixed.

Yellow Ochre: Very useful in colouring Plaster of Paris. Also used as a cheap water stain with size to bind it.

Below is the name and address of a high-class Polish Manufacturer which has a good reputation for high quality material. I must state that they will not supply you with quantities in pint sizes when purchasing French Polish or Methylated Spirit, only in 5 litre cans. However, if you mention my book they will allow you to purchase materials at trade price.

SONNEBORN & RIECK LIMITED
Jaxa Industrial Finishes,
91-95 Peregrine Road,
Hainault, Ilford,
Essex. IG6 3XH.
England.